8

VAN GOGH

AUVERS-SUR-OISE

PETITE ENCYCLOPÉDIE
DE L'ART

VAN GOGH

AUVERS-SUR-OISE

BY

FRANÇOIS MATHEY

TUDOR PUBLISHING CO.

NEW YORK

It was the madness of Van Gogh, as it is the folly of lovers, to be caught up in a fiery, passionate, relentless attempt to discover a self that ever invites yet always resists possession—folly perhaps, but, once tasted, a transcending obsession. "What each man is exactly no one will ever be able to tell," wrote Léon Bloy. "There are those who bow beneath their own soul as if it were too great for them to bear—there are countless numbers who live in forgetfulness of its very existence." The last few weeks of Van Gogh's despairing pursuit were to be lived out at Auvers-sur-Oise. He himself seemed to feel that the cause was lost. "There are circumstances," he said, "in which it is better to be the vanquished than the victor, better Prometheus than Jupiter."

Anxious to have his brother near at hand, in more normal surroundings than those of the hospital at Saint-Rémy, yet aware that the noise and excitement of life in Paris itself were obviously out of the question, Theo had at first asked Pissarro to take Vincent to his home at Éragny. It was Pissarro who, when Vincent van Gogh had arrived in Paris in 1886, had ini-

HORSE AND CART. LEAD PENCIL.

tiated him into the impressionist technique. Observing the passionate enthusiasm of the newcomer, Pissarro had then remarked, little realising the doubly prophetic purport of his words, that "he will either go mad, or leave the impressionists far behind." However, Theo's request failed to meet with the approval of Madame Pissarro who considered Van Gogh's possible influence on her children too great a risk to take. Pissarro therefore suggested Auvers-sur-Oise, the "Barbizon" of the impressionists, where the presence of Dr. Gachet, who was known both as a specialist in mental diseases and as a patron of the arts, would be a twofold advantage.

On May 21, 1890, Vincent arrived at Auvers and took board and lodging—at 3 francs 50 a day—at the Café Ravoux, Place de l'Espérance. "Auvers is a charming place," he wrote. "Among other things, there are lots of old thatched cottages, which are few and far between these days. Its beauty has a certain solemnity. This is the real countryside—typical and picturesque." He was immediately sensitive to the charm of the same scenes which had captivated Corot, Daubigny, Pissarro, Guillaumin, Cézanne and so many others before him. Dr. Gachet was an odd character, and from the start Vincent was drawn to this extravagant personality with his shock of red hair, his unpredictable moods, and his curious interest in chiromancy, phrenology and homeopathy. Well-known as an art-lover, he had been a regular frequenter of the "Nouvelle Athènes" and the Café Andler, and when he retired to Auvers in 1872 many of the artistic fraternity had followed him there. It is of little importance now to speculate as to whether Dr. Gachet had any real appreciation of the art of Van Gogh. One thing is certain, however—that he realised that he had to do with a man of genius. The Doctor's house in the Rue Rémy (now Rue des Vessenots) was always open to Van Gogh, who found there something approaching the warmth of a family circle. He painted the garden several times, portraits of the daughter of the house, Marguerite, among her flowers and at her piano (Pl. 6), and an astonishing portrait—after only two sittings—of the Doctor (Pl. 10). Gachet himself instructed him in the technique of etching.

Van Gogh, perhaps believing that he had found peace at last, worked with an enthusiasm that soon, however, increased to a pitch of frenzy.

No one can ever look out again over the peaceful skyline that surrounds Auvers without seeing the twisted, baroque, hallucinating landscapes of Van Gogh rise before his eyes. In two months he painted some seventy canvases. Some are happy and relaxed, suffused with greens and pinks, but most of them are terrifying, charged with forebodings of death, marked with the signs of the now inevitable catastrophe—like *The Cornfield with Crows* (Pl. 15) —or with an immense longing for peace and the deep call of the enfolding earth gently rocked by the caressing wind. He continued to work with tremendous energy, for now only work stood between him and insanity: "I use every ounce of my energy to master my work, telling myself that this is the best lightning-conductor for my afflictions." He was under no illusion when he wrote in a note to Theo found in his pocket after his death: "As for my work, I do it at my life's risk, and half my reason has foundered in it."

The first days in Auvers, however, had been encouraging. "I realize that it was good for me to go to the South. It has helped me to see the North more clearly. It is just as I had expected, I see purples, more where they really are. Auvers is certainly extremely beautiful," he wrote. Again, in a letter to his mother: "I am completely absorbed in the spectacle of these immense plains of cornfields stretching back to the hills, vast as the sea, tinged with a delicate yellow, a very pale green and a very soft mauve, bordered by strips of ploughed earth dotted with bushy potato plants in flower—all this under a blue sky with shades of white and pink and purple. I feel very much at peace, perhaps too much. I feel that I shall be able to paint this."

It was about this time that he painted those yew trees in Dr. Gachet's garden, which are so like the cypresses of Saint-Rémy, vibrant with a new-found joy in living, and also the portrait of Mademoiselle Gachet: "white roses, vine branches, and a white face in the midst." In early June he set up his easel by the apse of the little church in Auvers (Pl. 9). The baroque rhythm and violent colours of Van Gogh distort

DAUBIGNY'S GARDEN AT AUVERS. INK DRAWING.

the serene lines of the Gothic architecture and force them out of their balanced composure. He described it thus: "I have a better painting of a village church. The building appears shot with purple against a plain deep-blue sky of pure cobalt, the stained-glass windows appear as blue of ultramarine, the roof is purple with one part coloured orange. In the foreground, some foliage with flowers and pink sand in the sunlight. It is almost the same thing again as I did of the old tower and the cemetery at Neunen—only this time the colour is richer and more expressive."

He did numerous studies in the village—banked-up roadways, a street lined with houses,

LA BARGE. INK DRAWING.

THE MAIRIE AT AUVERS. LEAD PENCIL.

old man Pilon's house, and the farmhouse of old farmer Éloi. He felt strangely drawn to these primitive rustic surroundings, for they brought back the deep impressions that the cottages of Neunen had made on him in earlier days. The streets of Auvers were simply earth roadways filled with stones, leading straight out into the country—a silent, insistent call to the open plains, drowsy with the warmth of the sun and the promise of the harvest, under the deep, brilliant blue of the sky low overhead. Vincent's head seemed to swim at the prospect of these unending horizons—though we may note in passing that this awed preoccupation with perspectives that fade into infinity has always found an echo in the hearts of the Dutch and in the landscape painting of Holland since the time of Philippe de Koninck and Hobbema.

When he was tired after long periods in the open air, Van Gogh would come back to the village and call in at Dr. Gachet's. There he found still life subjects in abundance. And then, suddenly, there came back to him the old obsession for the portrait. The imperious, passionate search began again—to see a face (his own or the face of another) and fix it in his mind, seek out its hidden identity, and finally become its master. Beside this one obsession, all the rest, however serious, seemed mere entertainment. He must paint a portrait—for a portrait is a triumph over the secret that every man bears in his breast (Pl. 2). See the terrible fixed lucidity in the eyes, the twisted mouth. But the real enigma, the secret set in flame, once more lay just beyond his grasp. Failing with himself, he began the portrait of Dr. Gachet in white cap and blue jacket (Pl. 10). "What fires my most passionate interest," he wrote, "much, much more than anything else in painting, is the portrait, the modern portrait. I hope to discover the secret of it through colour, though I am certainly not alone in that. What I want, do you see, is this—I am far from pretending that I can achieve all these things, but am working towards them—I want to paint portraits which will give the impression to people a hundred years from now of the subject himself appearing before them, then and there. Obviously I don't attempt to do it through photographic resemblances, but rather through our own passionate expressions, using

WOMEN IN THE FIELDS. LEAD PENCIL.

as a mean of expressing and heightening the individual character our understanding of colour and the modern appeal of colour. In the portrait of Dr. Gachet, for example, the sunburned face is shown as a very very hot brick colour, the hair red, the cap white against a background of landscape and distant blue hills. The jacket is a deep ultramarine blue which makes the face stand out in contrast, and gives it a pale appearance in spite of its brick red. The hands—like the hands of a midwife —are paler than the face."

Van Gogh had, by then, been living in Auvers for almost a month. He was still on as cordial terms as ever with Dr. Gachet, but the two of

VAN GOGH ON HIS DEATH-BED,
BY DR. GACHET.

them had begun to have frequent, and often heated arguments, which had an adverse effect on Van Gogh's health and caused him little by little to lose his confidence in Gachet as his medical adviser. At the same time he felt himself losing his grip on his means of expression—his style became mechanical, his touch less sure and less sensitive. He was on the verge of a relapse. The recommendations of his doctor and discussions with his own family only served to exasperate him further. The conviction grew on him that he no longer meant anything to anyone—not even to Theo, who was now married and whose first child had just been born. And all the time the dread threat of insanity never left him. Desperately he clutched at the one remaining straw—always the same—his painting. On the 14th of July he painted the *Mairie at Auvers,* but the agitated uncertain touch, the twisted contours, even the proportions of the subject strangely elongated upwards, leave no doubt that the strain had almost reached breaking-point.

On the 27th of July he took a big canvas up to the high ground near Auvers to paint once more the endless cornfields that overlook the village. What happened there we do not know. Perhaps a sudden sense came over him of the futility of his efforts and of the meaninglessness of his existence. He fired a revolver bullet into his chest. The shot missed his heart and he was able to walk back to his room in the Café Ravoux. Theo was sent for, and two days later, on July 29th, Vincent died, saying in answer to his brother's attempts to comfort him: "It's no use—misery will never end."

LIST OF PLATES

4. ROAD NEAR AUVERS. JUNE 1890. *Pushkin Museum of Decorative Arts, Moscow.*

5. STREET AT AUVERS-SUR-OISE. JUNE 1890. *Atheneum Museum, Helsinki.*

6. MADEMOISELLE GACHET AT THE PIANO. JUNE 1890. *Kunstmuseum, Basle.*

7. COTTAGES AT CORDEVILLE. JUNE 1890. *The Louvre, Paris.*

8. GARDEN AND HOUSES. MAY-JUNE 1890. *Mme J. van Gogh-Bonger Collection, Amsterdam.*

9. THE CHURCH AT AUVERS. JUNE 1890. *The Louvre, Paris.*

10. PORTRAIT OF DR. GACHET. JUNE 1908. *The Louvre, Paris.*

11. STONE COTTAGES AT CHAPONVILLE. 1890. *Kunsthaus, Zurich.*

12. THE MAIRIE AT AUVERS ON JULY 14TH, 1890. *Private Collection, Chicago.*

13. PLAIN NEAR AUVERS. JUNE 1890. 19. *Jahrhunderts Gallery, Vienna.*

14. FIELD AND BLUE SKY. JULY 1890. *V. W. van Gogh Collection, Laren.*

15. CORNFIELD WITH CROWS. JULY 1890. *V. W. van Gogh Collection, Laren.*

I

4

5

6